TROUBLED

SOCIETY

DISCRIMINATION

Gregory Lee

The Rourke Corporation, Inc.
Vero Beach, Florida 32964

For Mr. Reed, Mr. Benson, and Mr. Boyce—
they told me I could.

The Rourke Corporation, Inc.
P.O. Box 3328, Vero Beach, FL 32964

Lee, Gregory, 1956-
    Discrimination / by Gregory Lee
        p. cm. — (Troubled society)
    Includes bibliographical references and index.
    Summary: Discusses the concept of prejudice; describes forms of discrimination based on race, sex, age, sexual preference, physical handicap, and appearance; and examines civil rights legislation.
    ISBN 0-86593-113-5
    1. Equality—United States—Juvenile literature. 2. Civil rights—United States—Juvenile literature. 3. Discrimination—United States—Juvenile literature. 4. Prejudices—United States—Juvenile literature. [1. Discrimination. 2. Prejudices. 3. Civil rights. 4. Equality.] I. Title. II. Series.
HM146.L38   1991
305—dc20   91-12175
                                                                             CIP
                                                                              AC

Series Editor: Gregory Lee
Editors: Elizabeth Sirimarco, Marguerite Aronowitz
Book design and production: The Creative Spark,
    Capistrano Beach, CA
Cover photograph: Jon Feingersh/Tom Stack & Associates

Contents

ONE

UNALIENABLE RIGHTS

Thomas Jefferson once composed the most famous and significant words in American history:

We hold these truths to be self-evident, that all men are created equal, that they are endowed by their Creator with certain unalienable Rights, that among these are Life, Liberty and the pursuit of Happiness.

When Jefferson wrote that sentence in the Declaration of Independence, he meant that there are certain areas of life that should never be controlled by anyone other than you—the individual. Every person has the right to live, be free, and follow their own dreams. Jefferson called this right *unalienable*, which means this freedom cannot be forfeited (given up) or transferred to someone else.

United States citizens are expected to accept this philosophy and live by it. Over the centuries our country has swelled with immigrants from many nations who also want to live by this code of freedom. We have even fought wars over these words—against people in distant countries.

But some Americans claim that when Jefferson's words were written, they did not include everyone. Women and slaves, for example, were certainly not "created equal" in the eyes of the men who formed our government. In the 200 years that followed the American Revolution, many new amendments had to be added to the Constitution to make these rights clearly apply to all citizens. That's because some citizens

Thomas Jefferson.

lacked what is called "equal opportunity." Throughout much of our history, minorities, women and members of certain religions have been prevented from sharing in the "American Dream," the dream of freedom and prosperity. Why? Because they faced *discrimination*.

Discrimination is the act or policy of treating someone differently, setting them apart, or denying them their rights, simply because they are different from the majority. For example, if a black man isn't given a job because of his race, he is being discriminated against. He's not being turned down because of his skills, ability, intelligence or past job experience, but simply because the company doesn't want to hire a black man.

The Equal Protection Clause

The problem of equal protection under the law was supposed to have been solved back in 1868, when the 14th Amendment was added to the United States Constitution. The 14th Amendment provides individuals with the legal ammunition for fighting discrimination. Section 1 of the amendment includes this passage:

> *No State shall make or enforce any law which shall abridge* [restrict] *the privileges or immunities of citizens of the United States; nor shall any State deprive any person of life, liberty or property, without due process of law; nor deny to any person within its jurisdiction the equal protection of the laws.*

This means that no one can be denied the rights all of us take for granted as citizens of the United States. Those rights are spelled out in the *Bill of Rights*, the first ten amendments to the Constitution. The last part of this passage is well-known as the *equal protection clause*. It means that all of us are affected by our laws, no matter who we are, how much money we earn, or the color of our skin.

There are no exceptions. That is, there aren't supposed to be any exceptions. But in the real world there are exceptions, because laws cannot always change personal emotions or attitudes. So people who believe they have been discriminated against have gone to court to try to enforce their right to equal protection. The equal protection clause has been the basis for nearly all discrimination lawsuits.

Today, people who believe they have been victims of discrimination on the job can file a complaint with the *Equal Employment Opportunity Commission* (EEOC), a federally-run program created in 1964. The complaint must be filed within 180 days of the act that an employee believes was or is discriminatory. The EEOC will investigate and, if there is a state or local agency that enforces discrimination laws, the complaint will be sent to them for consideration. Meanwhile, the EEOC determines whether the complaint is valid. If the decision is yes, it will inform the person of their rights.

People who can prove discrimination have several choices. They may sue their employer to make them change their policy, or they may get the EEOC to sue on their behalf. Sometimes the EEOC will sue on behalf of many employees at once, if the policy of discrimination has been widespread. This is known as a *class action suit.* If the employee or employees win the case, the court will order the employer to satisfy the employee or employees with actions that remove the effects of the discrimination. This might include payment of back pay and lost benefits, reinstating an employee or promoting them, and/or changing company policy to make sure the discrimination is not repeated.

The EEOC reviews discrimination cases because it is the federal agency responsible for enforcing Title VII of the Civil Rights Act of 1964. This law was passed to make it illegal for employers to discriminate on the

basis of "sex, race, color, religion, or national origin."
On the job, discrimination can occur in policies regarding hiring and firing, wages, benefits, promotions, and job training.

Who Suffers From Discrimination?

Throughout the history of the United States, those who have suffered the most from discrimination have usually been:

- New immigrants, who have trouble speaking English and may not immediately adopt "American" lifestyles;

- Blacks, who were enslaved for centuries before slavery was abolished during the Civil War of 1860-65;

- Native American Indians, who were killed and restricted for centuries until the few who remained were forced to live on public lands called "reservations";

- Women, who only gained the right to vote 70 years ago, and who are still scarce in the decision-making bodies of our government and in business; and

- The disabled, or handicapped, who until 1990 had few laws that gave them equal access to the rights and privileges most of us take for granted.

Society has recently become more aware of discrimination against older people, who often have difficulty finding employment even though many still want to work. This is age discrimination, or *agism*. People who are homosexual are also often victims of discrimination because of their sexual preference.

Many of those who immigrated to the United

States in the past 200 years had suffered from discrimination in their native countries. Some belonged to the wrong political group, or their religion was unpopular. Others became *refugees*: people who flee their native lands when political conflicts and wars take away their rights. Millions found that the United States offered more freedom and less discrimination, but less discrimination is not the same as *no* discrimination.

A long-established group of Americans have claimed recently that they have been victims of discrimination. They are winning some of their battles in court, and creating more confusion than ever about the legal methods invented to cure discrimination. Who are they? White males, who believe they are now paying the price for discrimination inflicted upon earlier generations of minorities.

Employers who have contracts with government agencies must demonstrate that they are "equal opportunity employers." This means they have to show that they hire and promote women and minorities on a regular basis. Some firms have met this requirement by picking a specific minimum number of job positions that must be filled by people from these previously disadvantaged groups. Critics have labeled this kind of hiring practice the *quota* system. They also call it unfair, because it uses race or gender as a substitute for good job qualifications. This is a debate that is still not settled, and will be discussed further in a later chapter.

Is it possible to have a "color blind" society? Maybe, but only when the cause of discrimination disappears: human prejudice.

TWO

IS PREJUDICE A SOCIAL DISEASE?

When you get the measles you get symptoms like a rash and fever. The uncomfortable symptoms are caused by the illness in your body. If you think of discrimination as the symptom of an illness, then prejudice would be the virus that causes it. *Prejudice* means to "pre-judge," to form an opinion based on little or no information. This judgment is usually based on suspicion, and that leads to fear. And fear creates a hostile attitude that springs from a natural urge to defend oneself against that fear.

To simplify it a bit, think of one form of prejudice as the fear of "not like us." For example, the fear of strangers—especially if their appearance or lifestyle is different from ours—seems almost instinctive. This instinct may come from our prehistoric origins. Among animals in nature, to fear "not like us" is a strategy for survival, like the old joke about "shoot first and ask questions later." It may mean attacking a predator before it can attack you. Early humans probably survived by taking such precautions. They didn't think about their fear, they simply reacted.

This protective urge is still strong today, especially in the defense of one's home and family. For example, an intruder climbing into your bedroom window is a threat to your security, and is not welcome. You would naturally protect your home.

Prejudice is like this, except it can be a negative judgment or reaction against another person based on a lack of knowledge about them. It can be dislike and distrust based only on appearance or other differences

The three lawyers who argued before the Supreme Court against segregation in public schools were (left to right) George E.C. Hayes, Thurgood Marshall (later named associate justice), and James M. Nabrit.

("not like us"), and not on any factual information about who they are or what they want.

So, like a virus in the human body, prejudice is at the root of many social illnesses all around the world. Countries as varied as the Soviet Union, South Africa, Northern Ireland, Lebanon and India have had riots, bombings, executions and open warfare because people in those countries have ethnic and religious differences. Their ignorance and fear of each other disrupts their lives as they seek revenge for real or imagined wrongs against their own kind. This fear becomes a vicious cycle, feeding on itself and passing pain and suffering from one generation to the next.

Discrimination in the social sense happens most often when people with power or government authority deny another person his or her rights simply because that person is different. Whether we realize it or not, when we're young our parents, teachers, television shows, and friends pass along many feelings and beliefs to us. We often accept them as being true. If these beliefs are prejudiced, however, we grow up believing things about people we've never met that may not be true at all. This is unfair. No one should be judged blindly. Unfortunately, many people don't want to listen to other ideas that challenge their beliefs. But by exposing these narrow beliefs, we can see prejudice for what it is: the excuse for discrimination.

Freedom of Association

If the Constitution prohibits discrimination, why is it still a problem? The answer is that we as cit-

This protest on the Mills College campus was unusual because the protesters were not protesting to eliminate discrimination. Instead, the students at this all-female college were protesting a decision to admit males to their school.

izens can't agree on the meaning of "equal protection" under the law. Even our courts can't make up their minds. With every new lawsuit and court decision, the signs and cures of discrimination seem to become more confusing.

For example, there is something called the "freedom of association." Everyone likes to be with people they like and avoid people they don't like. The desire of people to be separate from others for personal reasons is very human. To be separate, however, does not necessarily mean to be *segregated*. Segregation

A Gap In Perceptions

A 1990 Gallup Poll revealed these wide differences of opinion about equal opportunity in America. Here are the percentages of people who agreed with the following statements:

Blacks have as good a chance as whites:	Respondents White	Black
To get any kind of job for which they are qualified.	73%	43%
To get any kind of housing they can afford.	75	47
To get a good education.	85	68

And consider the percentage of blacks and whites who said "yes" to these statements:

	White	Black
Quality of life for blacks has gotten better.	62	46
Quality of life for blacks has gotten worse.	6	23
American society as a whole is more tolerant.	54	29

means to *enforce* separation between groups, which will be discussed in the next chapter.

In the same spirit, some people join clubs where all the members have something in common. For example, there are clubs for military veterans, people in similar businesses or hobbies, single parents, off-road cyclists—clubs of all kinds. Often these clubs have rules about who is allowed to join and who is not. The members believe they should be allowed to associate with whomever they want. After all, if just anybody can join, what's the purpose of having a "club"? So it seems logical that club members don't want to have everyone in the world as a member. Is this what is meant by the phrase "freedom of association"?

Certain clubs have been criticized for their strict rules about who can and who cannot be a member. Usually they have been "all-white" clubs or "all-male" clubs (sometimes both). If members of minorities tried to join all-white clubs, or women tried to join all-male clubs, they were turned down. Is this freedom of association, or discrimination?

Since the government enforces our laws, agencies and programs run by the government are expected to have antidiscrimination policies. But if a club or activity is private, then what the members do is their own business, as long as it harms no one else, right? After all, private clubs don't prevent blacks or Hispanics from voting in an election. They don't keep illiterate people from getting jobs. They don't deny women the right to become steelworkers. Club members often believe that "equal protection" should only apply to public agencies and policies.

Los Angeles attorney Gloria Allred displays her Friars Club membership card after winning her court battle to be admitted to the formerly all-male club.

The courts have ruled that clubs are not always immune from antidiscrimination laws just because they call themselves "private." In the 1980s, for example, a Los Angeles attorney sued a men's club known as the Friars Club for barring women from membership. Since the club was for businessmen only, the female attorney argued that by refusing her membership, she could not take advantage of business contacts made by male club members. The males benefited because they were able to meet new business clients. The attorney won her lawsuit, and now the Friars Club is no longer all-male. The fact that the club was "private" and not "public" did not protect it from antidiscrimination laws.

In 1990, the Professional Golfer's Association of America (PGA of America) was embarrassed by news reports that it had scheduled a tournament at an all-white country club in Alabama. The PGA of America later told the Shoal Creek Country Club that it could not host the championship golf event unless the club began accepting minorities as members. The club changed its policy, and a local black businessman became its first minority member. Such a breakthrough seems like a case of "too little, too late," but this change in membership would have been impossible 40 years ago. It turns out that many other country clubs that host golf tournaments have similar policies, but they have never been challenged. If more pro golf tours refused to hold their profitable tournaments at clubs that discrminate, many might find their business will suffer.

DESEGREGATION AND AFFIRMATIVE ACTION

All minorities in America have had to fight their share of discrimination and prejudice, but none have had to fight as long and hard as African-Americans. Most black people in the United States were legally slaves until 1863, when President Lincoln issued the *Emancipation Proclamation*, formally declaring all slaves to be free men and women. But by the end of the Civil War in 1865, things hadn't improved much. Many blacks remained poor farm laborers and factory workers, having scarcely any more rights than they had as slaves. In many areas of the country it took blacks another 100 years before they were given the right to vote, own property, and attend decent schools.

Late in the 1950s, the *civil rights movement* grew out of the southern states, where discrimination based on skin color was most obvious. "Whites only" was a sign posted at restaurants, public restrooms, drinking fountains, laundromats, bus stops, and countless other places. Most hotels did not accept black guests. Voter "poll taxes" and literacy "tests" were tricks used to keep blacks from voting in many local elections where whites were a minority of the population.

Then one by one, lawsuits brought by black people led the courts to strike down many laws as discriminatory. But despite the court rulings many rights were still denied to black people. Discriminatory practices were unwritten rules of conduct.

Rosa Parks was fined $14 for failing to move to the segregated section of a Montgomery, Alabama, city bus. The incident triggered a boycott of the municipal bus system, and led to a widespread civil rights movement.

In 1955, Rosa Parks violated a local ordinance when she refused to ride in the back of a public bus in Montgomery, Alabama. She was arrested. This single event triggered a bus *boycott*, and eventually the bus company in Montgomery lost so many riders that it had to give in and allow black people to sit anywhere they wanted. The civil rights movement grew rapidly, and for years to come both blacks and whites marched in cities across the United States in favor of civil rights. They demanded an end to seg- regation, and worked for fair treatment of all people, regardless of skin color.

It may be hard for today's young people to imagine the turmoil that was stirred up by the civil rights movement. Americans in large numbers protested the unfair treatment of blacks. Young white men and women from northern states traveled to the South to help with voter registration of blacks. They participated in marches, and were arrested alongside black people. They wanted to show the rest of the country that not all Americans were being treated equally. Many white people were beaten savagely, and some disappeared. A few were killed outright—the victims of angry whites who resented other people (especially from the north) telling them how to treat black people.

In 1957, National Guardsmen were called in by the governor of Arkansas to bar nine black students from enrolling in all-white Central High School in Little Rock. But when a federal court ordered their removal, the state gave in. When the black students came to school on September 23, they were told to leave for their own safety. A huge mob had gathered around the school to taunt the blacks and threaten them.

The very next day President Eisenhower sent federal troops into Little Rock to enforce the court order, allowing the black students to attend Central High. It seems incredible to us now to think that anyone would need the protection of armed troops just to attend school, but that was America in 1957.

The movement reached its peak when Congress passed the Civil Rights Act of 1964 and the Voting Rights Act of 1965. These new federal laws made it unlawful to discriminate on the basis of "sex,

Federal troops were necessary in 1957 to enforce the Supreme Court's ban on segregated schools in many southern states. Here, African-American students are escorted home from Central High School in Little Rock, Arkansas.

race, color, religion, or national origin." No one can be fired, underpaid, denied promotion, or lose any other benefits or privileges just because they belong to the "wrong" ethnic group or gender.

Desegregation

In one of the most important civil rights cases in United States history, the Supreme Court ruled 9-0 that schools with separate or *segregated* student bodies were unconstitutional. The court rejected the idea that schools could be "separate but equal." All-black schools were not equal in quality because they had less money, poorer facilities, and inferior classroom materials. The Supreme Court said that segregation violated the 14th Amendment, and school districts were ordered to *integrate* (blend) schools so that black and white children attended together. Between 1968 and 1972, there was a 59 percent increase in the number of black children attending school alongside whites in the South.

The most common way to integrate schools was to put children on school buses and take them to either all-white or all-black schools out of their own neighborhoods. This method, called "busing," was immediately controversial. Many white parents objected to their children being forced to attend schools far from their homes. Supporters said that parents who resisted busing were showing their true feelings about race—that they didn't like busing because they didn't like integration. So many white parents moved their families out of school districts with court-ordered busing programs that this phe-nomenon received a nickname: "white flight."

In cities nationwide there were endless court challenges to court-ordered busing, but the practice became widespread in many school districts. The furor gradually died down and, as a result, many children of the '70s and '80s are no longer strangers to children of other colors in school. Opinions differ, however, about whether integration had the desired effect on minority education. For example, today the number of black males who enroll in and finish col-lege still lags significantly behind other ethnic groups.

In 1991 the Supreme Court ruled that court-ordered desegregation programs are not permanent, and can be ended when the separation of students by race has been halted. In a 5-3 vote, the court said that if a school board has "complied in good faith" with a desegregation order in all practical ways, then the order or decree should be dropped.

Court-ordered busing was meant only "as a temporary measure," according to Chief Justice William Rehnquist. According to the court, equal treatment does not mean a judge has to oversee public school policy forever. The court also said that a school board may return to a policy of neighborhood schools, even if the schools that were once all-minorities become that way again. Similarly, schools in white neighborhoods could become all-white again.

It is too soon to tell what effect this will have on schools as we approach the year 2000. It appears that the Supreme Court now believes that "separate but equal" is no longer unconstitutional.

Affirmative Action

Early attempts to eliminate discrimination in the American workplace and on college campuses did not do away with friction between minorities and whites. Despite the legislation of the 1960s, by 1970 it was clear that minorities and women were still not filling "white collar" jobs at the rate of white males. Women made up over one-half of the population, but they still remained mostly workers, not bosses. The same is true today. Among America's top 500 corporations, less than two percent of the top executives are female.

Martin Luther King, Jr. once said that in the foot race for equality, the minority person would just have to run faster. But in the 1970s, many experts—including some Supreme Court justices—believed it wasn't a fair race. They felt that generations of discrimination had set minorities back so far that whites (and especially white males) had a head start in any job race. That was when the concept of *affirmative action* was born.

Companies and colleges were encouraged to take a closer look at minority applicants and be aggressive about giving them job placement and promotions. Eventually many companies who wanted to do business with the federal government were required to prove they had affirmative action programs. The companies created guidelines—literally, how many people of color (or gender) they should hire per year to meet their goals.

Critics say that this system means hiring people based upon *quotas* or *set asides*—merely filling a set number of positions without regard for the best-qualified person for the job. Some working people say they have lost jobs, promotions or contracts because an affirmative action policy pushed their qualifications aside in favor of a minority. These critics call it *reverse discrimination*: same disease, new victim.

In his 1991 State of the Union speech, President Bush labeled these policies "unfair preferences." The change in wording is significant, because voters react to words. And when politicians talk to voters, their words are crafted to match the views of their audience. To his listeners, the president's words meant, "No one should be *given* a job just because of their gender or skin color." In the

When people attempted to integrate public places, like this Jackson, Mississippi lunch counter, crowds of people jeered. These protesters had ketchup, mustard, and sugar poured over their heads.

days during the civil rights movement, the more popular phrase would've been, "No one should be *denied* a job just because of their gender or skin color."

Although there is just one word changed in these two sentences, it alters the meaning quite a bit. The affirmative action debate is over which meaning is more just. Does one word make such a difference?

Yes, because some people believe that an affirmative action policy *denies* a job to some—

namely, *white* people—by giving a job to members of minorities. If two people are equally qualified for a job or promotion, and a minority gets the position, the non-minority might feel he or she was a victim of reverse discrimination.

In a tight labor market, where there are more workers than job openings, affirmative action will have a definite impact. If one person is hired because a company must meet a hiring goal based on race or gender, then another person is also denied a job on the same grounds. Is this discrimination? Apparently the Supreme Court of the latter 1980s and early 1990s has begun to agree.

In 1978 a student named Allan Bakke claimed he was denied a place in a University of California medical school because he was white. The school had set aside 16 out of 100 new admission slots for people of color. Bakke argued that his test scores were better than some of the minority students who had been accepted. He claimed discrimination. The Supreme Court ruled that Bakke should have been admitted.

In a 1989 decision, white firefighters in Birmingham, Alabama, claimed that they were victims of reverse discrimination because of a court order. Black firefighters were to be promoted until they were closer in number to the proportion of blacks in the local labor force. The white firefighters said this was a quota system, and unfair. Again, the Supreme Court agreed.

Those who support affirmative action feel that these judgments are hasty reversals of important public policy. Without strong affirmative action programs, supporters say, our society will backslide into the mistakes of the past. Some people believe that affirmative action must continue to make up for past discrimination; that is, try to compensate for the decades of lost opportunities based on gender or skin color.

Since many decisions of the late 1980s appeared to weaken affirmative action policies, legislators in Congress recently wrote a bill to try to reverse the effects of these Supreme Court decisions. The Civil Rights Act of 1990 was passed by Congress, but it was vetoed by President Bush because he said it would restore the "quota" solution to discrimination. The Senate failed to override his veto by a single vote.

Is Affirmative Action Effective?

Has affirmative action corrected past hiring abuses? Read these statistics and judge:

- Only six percent of managerial jobs belong to black Americans (but blacks make up more than 12 percent of the total U.S. population).
- Lawyers and accountants are highly paid professionals. To be a partner in a law or accounting firm is an honor worth many extra thousands of dollars in salary per year. But at the nation's 250 largest law firms, less than one percent of the law partners are black. In accounting, one-quarter of one percent of the partners are black.
- Blacks make up only four percent of the nation's newspaper and magazine journalists.
- Blacks earn 10 to 26 percent less than whites with similar educational backgrounds.

Thoughts On Prejudice

Treat all men alike. Give them all the same laws. Give them all an even chance to live and grow.
        —*Chief Joseph, Nez Perce Indian leader*

I am free of all prejudices. I hate every one equally.
        —*W.C. Fields, comedian*

I have a dream that my four little children will one day live in a nation where they will not be judged by the color of their skin but by the content of their character.
        —Martin Luther King, Jr., civil rights leader

Those who deny freedom to others deserve it not for themselves.
        —*Abraham Lincoln, 16th President of the United States*

If we were to wake up some morning and find that everyone was the same race, creed and color, we would find some other causes for prejudice by noon.
        —*George Aiken, former U.S. senator*

It is never too late to give up your prejudices.
        —*Henry David Thoreau, American philosopher*

There is no more evil thing in this world than race prejudice.
        —*H.G. Wells, author and historian*

A black author and professor of English from a California university has recently criticized minorities, saying they now use affirmative action like a crutch. Shelby Steele believes that by accepting preferences or quotas, black people are admitting they can't succeed as well as white people.

"I think those policies rob the entire race of their power," says Steele. "What the civil rights movement wanted was a fair and equal society... Affirmative action, it seems to me, does the opposite of that.

"When you give preferences to blacks, you make it look as though everybody else made it on merit and [blacks] made it on color." Steele says bluntly that minorities must stop relying on special legal advantages and prove they are just as good as any person based on merit. Anything less, Steele says, surrenders power and dignity and breeds ugly stereotypes instead.

FOUR

THE PLIGHT OF WOMEN

Throughout history, women have worked just as hard as men to maintain their families and homes. In the past women were considered to be inferior to men, and their only role in society was to bear and raise children. They were expected to provide comfort and care for their mates as well. As Americans moved west, women had as much work to do as ever: building homes, keeping their families healthy and fed, and working on farms and ranches—doing work as difficult as any man's job.

During the Great Depression of the 1930s, many women had to extend their workdays outside the home. They worked at jobs for pennies an hour to help their families survive. During World War II, the nation's factories were full of women building weapons, ships and planes for the men fighting the war. Women managed to accomplish the tough jobs once thought of as "men's work." But when the war ended, the men returned to their jobs and the women were sent home.

It was during the post-war *baby boom* between 1946 and 1964, when the birth rate skyrocketed, that many women grew dissatisfied with their lives. They saw themselves as being stuck in the house, raising children, cleaning and cooking for the family, and making life pleasant for their husband and children. They had no identity other than that of wife and mother.

Women At Work

The one-income family finally began to disap-

These women marched down New York's Fifth Avenue for women's suffrage in 1918. The 19th Amendment was passed in 1920, declaring that women had the right to vote.

pear during the 1970s and '80s. Many women wanted their own careers. They wanted to get the education formerly denied them. They wanted some independence. That's when the *feminist* or women's liberation movement was born. Before the 1970s, women who worked outside the home were usually teachers, nurses, secretaries or telephone operators. These were called "pink collar" jobs. Often these jobs came with a lot of responsibility but little recognition and small salaries.

Another reason that more and more women began to enter the work force is that they had no choice. The growing U.S. economy increased prices but shrank incomes. It took two adults working full-time at well-paying careers to maintain the same lifestyle that many middle-class Americans had taken for granted.

The problem of discrimination has been an ever-present obstacle for women. They are not even specifically mentioned in the Constitution. In the 1970s, females around the country tried to correct this by fighting for the Equal Rights Amendment (ERA). The ERA would have made it illegal to discriminate based on gender, but it was never ratified by enough states to become law.

Women gained the right to vote in 1920, only a little over 70 years ago, when the 19th Amendment was passed. They make up 51 percent of the total population, yet men still hold most of the country's political offices. Out of 535 possible seats in Congress, fewer than 30 are held by women. Less than 11 percent of mayors nationwide are women, and less than one percent are heads of all the fire or police departments in America.

Today, women are filling more "white collar" jobs, and they hold more traditionally "male" jobs than ever before. But they must prove again and again that they can do a job "as well as a man." Many employers once believed that women were not as strong, dedicated or determined as a man, and that they weren't tough enough to succeed in business. Many women have proved that stereotype wrong, yet their salaries don't reflect equality. On average, women still make 70 cents for every dollar a man earns. This is due partly to more women being in lower-paying occupations, however the "salary gap" is slowly shrinking due to younger

Women are still excluded from certain "male" fields—in this case, the baseball field. Pam Postema, a minor league umpire, was refused a spot on the National League umpire roster in 1989.

women entering the workplace with better educations and training than their mothers had.

Many working women have had to file lawsuits to earn *equal pay*—the same amount a man does for the same job. Furthermore, many women claim that traditional "women's" jobs are undervalued in the job market, paying less than they should. These women support the practice of *comparable worth*: paying similar salaries for jobs that are judged equally as tough as many "men's" jobs. This issue is not easily resolved, and isn't likely to be any time soon.

Many women in the workplace have experienced what has been called the "glass ceiling," the transparent barrier that keeps a female from rising to the top of her profession because males won't promote them. For example, Nancy Ezold was a candidate for a partnership in a Philadelphia law firm in 1988. While three fellow male lawyers who were after the same post all received poor recommendations, Ezold was described as having "guts and maturity" and called "exceptionally good." She didn't receive the promotion, however—one of her male competitors did.

When Ezold took her case to court, a federal district judge agreed that she was the victim of *sexual discrimination*. The law firm was ordered to pay her compensation. This case was only one in a series that reconfirmed that Title VII of the 1964 Civil Rights Act applies to all. Yet today, many corporations, universities, and professional firms continue to ignore qualified women employees in favor of men. Increasingly, these employers are being forced by pressure from women's groups and the courts to make a permanent change in their "business as usual" policies that discriminate against women.

Sexual Harassment

Sometimes discrimination takes another form when women are denied the right to job interviews, promotions, salary raises and reviews because they ignore the sexual advances of a boss or co-worker. There have been many instances where women were told outright that unless they had sex with their employer, they would not receive the consideration they were entitled to as good employees. They could even be fired.

Threatening an employee with loss of their job if they don't grant sexual favors is called *sexual harassment*. A female employee may sue her employer if she is a victim of this treatment. When a female employee is denied some benefit because she isn't open to sexual advances, she is the victim of discrimination. In these cases, the discrimination is the result not of who the employee is, but what she won't do. More women than ever before are standing up to this kind of discrimination, although many complain that sexual harassment is far from extinct in the American workplace.

Fetal Protection Policies

A recent wrinkle in female discrimination appeared in the past 10 years in the form of "fetal protection laws." Some large companies—including General Motors and Du Pont—excluded their female employees from certain jobs because of their physical

Millions of American women work on assembly lines in "blue-collar" jobs, and many have had to fight discrimination to earn the same pay and benefits as male employees.

ability to become pregnant. These companies feared that exposure to harmful substances like lead, which may cause birth defects, could potentially harm any children born to their female employees in the future. To protect themselves from lawsuits, these companies restricted jobs with hazardous exposure to men only. The only way a woman could hold such a job was to prove that she had been *sterilized* (a medical procedure that prevents a woman from getting pregnant).

In a March 1991 ruling, however, the Supreme Court struck down all fetal protection policies as clearly discriminatory. "Decisions about the welfare of future children must be left to the parents who conceive, bear, support and raise them, rather than to the employers who hire those parents," wrote Justice Harry A. Blackmun. In this specific case, the court decided that a concern for a women's potential offspring was being used by Johnson Control (a battery manufacturer) to deny women equal employment opportunities. Johnson Control argued that it was only concerned with worker health and safety, but the court ruled 6-3 that warning employees of the potential danger of harmful on-the-job exposure was as far as the company could go.

One factor in the women workers' favor was that the connection between birth defects and the parents is still not clearly understood. Very little research has been done on the contribution of the male in conception to any birth defects. Males who are exposed to toxic substances on a regular basis can sometimes become *infertile* (unable to produce enough sperm to conceive a child). Since this fact has been documented, it is possible that sperm could be a source of future birth defects just as much as a female's egg. Therefore, it was unfair of businesses to assume that the only way to prevent birth defects (and future lawsuits) was to stop women from working in hazardous areas.

Millions of women are expected to benefit from this Supreme Court decision, as thousands of jobs are once again open to them.

FIVE

DISABLED, GAY, UGLY, AND OLD

In July 1990, President Bush signed into law the Americans with Disabilities Act (ADA). This bill expanded civil rights protections to an estimated 43 million handicapped persons. The law fills in some gaps in the Civil Rights Act of 1964 and the Rehabilitation Act of 1973 so that they include handicapped people in present antidiscrimination policies.

The Rehabilitation Act made equal opportunity rules apply to any federal program or institution that receives federal funds. The ADA makes all cities and towns comply with rules in hiring and *structural accessibility* (buildings must be designed with handicapped people in mind).

Many handicapped people cannot use the same public facilities that others take for granted. This is because many public areas—from restaurants to subways to movie theaters—lack convenient facilities that permit people in wheelchairs to enter, exit and enjoy them. For example, the physical height of drinking fountains, pay telephones, urinals and other features in public areas has to be planned for people in wheelchairs. And Braille instructions in elevators and at automatic teller machines help sightless people use them as easily as others do.

In employment, many people with disabilities in vision, hearing, speech or movement are denied work, even though they can perform many of the same jobs as those without disabilities. Others can perform jobs if minor changes are made to accom-

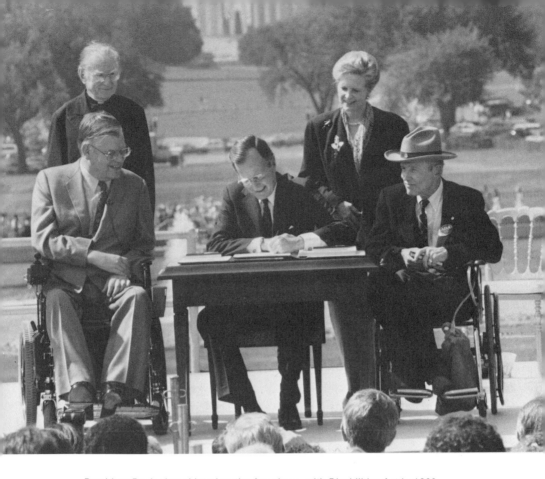

President Bush signed into law the Americans with Disabilities Act in 1990.
Evan Kemp, chairman of the Equal Employment Opportunity Commission
(left, seated), and Justin Dart, chairman of the President's Council on
Disabilities (right, seated), attended the ceremony.

modate them. For example, a paralyzed person can now operate a computer terminal by directing a light on the screen. The light is placed on the operator's head, like a pair of glasses.

For a long time, telephones were useless to people who were deaf or hearing-impaired. Now, however, technology has made it possible for people to receive messages using a telecommunications device for the deaf (called a TDD). A hearing-impaired person is equipped with a special device on which he or she can type a message. The message is then sent over the phone line to a special operator who can relay the call to whomever the caller wishes to contact. The system works in reverse, too, so that a person can also receive messages through a TDD. Fax machines and computer modems are other technical improvements that help members of the deaf community keep in touch. Handicapped Americans have made perhaps the strongest headway against discrimination of any minority group in recent years.

Fear Of Disease

People with infectious diseases are often victims of discrimination because people around them fear they will catch the disease. This has affected the *homosexual* or gay community more than most, because the spread of AIDS was, at first, significantly higher among gays. Many people believe they will get AIDS simply by being near someone who has HIV (*human immunodeficiency virus*—the virus that causes the disease). They are mistaken. The U.S. Surgeon General has stated the few specific ways that people can get AIDS, and just being close to someone with AIDS will not infect anyone. Yet people have lost their jobs when employers learned they had HIV. Sadly, this means they often hide their disease for fear of losing their jobs (or not being hired). Some people with HIV are even afraid to get needed medical attention because they fear discrimination.

A tragic example of this is Ryan White, who was 14 years old when he contracted HIV from a

These children protested the attendance of young Ryan White at their school when it was learned he had the AIDS virus. Their parents were afraid they would contract AIDS too.

blood transfusion. When his infection was discovered, parents with children attending the same school as Ryan in Kokomo, Indiana, began protesting. They didn't want their children exposed to Ryan. The White family moved to Illinois to get away from the hostile circumstances, and eventually won their right to put Ryan in any school. Ryan, who became a modest and brave spokesman about AIDS, died in 1990.

Homosexual Discrimination

People who are homosexual continue to face discrimination in the United States. In some states, homosexuality (choosing to have sexual relations with a person of the same gender) is still against the law, although these laws are rarely enforced. If someone is technically breaking the law, however, it makes it easier to deprive them of their rights. For example, convicted criminals are imprisoned and deprived of their liberty and right to vote until they are released.

Gays And The Military

During the Persian Gulf War, a Navy admiral sent a memo to his commanders stating that more should be done to identify and discharge *lesbians* (female homosexuals) from the Navy. He complained that the service tolerated lesbians more than male homosexuals. In an ironic choice of words the admiral wrote, "Demonstrate equality in the treatment of male and female homosexuals. The problem won't just go away, so we must deal with it sensibly, and fairly, with due regard for the privacy

These people are participating in the Gay and Lesbian Pride March in New York City. Even in the 1990s, many homosexuals conceal their sexual preferences in order to avoid discrimination.

interests of all." In other words, all gays should be discriminated against equally. They should not be allowed to defend their country.

Why would an admiral utter such harsh words? Doesn't he know we're trying to rid our society of discrimination? Should the military have different rules? It is interesting that in 1990, the U.S. Supreme Court refused to hear an appeal to overturn the military's no-homosexual policy.

Former Army Reserve drill sergeant Miriam Ben-Shalom was discharged from the Army because she is a lesbian. According to Pentagon regulations, "homosexual conduct seriously impairs the accom-

Television news anchor Christine Craft flashes victory outside a Missouri federal court after winning her discrimination lawsuit against the station that fired her when she refused to alter her appearance for the cameras.

plishment of the military mission." How? By supposed-ly undermining discipline, order and morale. Cur-rently the Pentagon discharges about 1,000 men and women every year for being gay. This policy was reinforced in 1991 when a Pentagon official said, "Homosexuality is incompatible with military service." When Ben-Shalom and other gays took their case to the Supreme Court, their appeal was unsuccessful.

Are there some practices of society—such as a person's choice of a sex partner—that should be immune to laws against discrimination? If the majori-ty believes that homosexuality is wrong, bad or immoral, does the majority have the right to discrimi-nate against homosexuals? If we say that all discrim-ination is wrong, should we be allowed to make exceptions? It appears that whether or not we should, we do. Discrimination based on a person's sexual preference is one barrier that Americans are not yet ready to tear down.

Beauty And Discrimination

Our society pays a lot of money for beauty. Cosmetics are a multi-billion-dollar industry. Television ads are filled with slim, handsome people, and dieting is a national obsession. But can being overweight cost you a job?

It can. Says one career counselor, "The most common assumption is that overweight people could be thin if they really wanted to...from that the con-clusion follows that if you're overweight, you're out of control." Would you hire a person who was out of control?

In 1990 the Association of Professional Flight

Attendants sued American Airlines for its policy on weight limits for women. For example, flight attendants who are five-feet, five-inches tall cannot weigh more than 129 pounds. The women employees said this amounted to sex discrimination. In 1989, Pan Am lost a similar suit and the judge awarded the flight attendants $2 million. Such lawsuits are rare, however, and only one state—Michigan—has a law that specifically prohibits weight discrimination.

Some employers who fight charges of weight discrimination argue that severe weight problems (*obesity*) may be a physical handicap for certain jobs, and certain courts have agreed. But now that discrimination against the handicapped has been weakened by the Americans with Disabilities Act, this may be a poor defense.

There are no laws, however, that prohibit discrimination based upon human opinions about attractiveness. An applicant for a sales job may be turned down because the interviewer thinks he or she is ugly. Is this fair? Should a company be afraid of losing business because one of its account managers is unattractive? How would someone prove they lost a job or promotion due to ugliness?

One well publicized case of "beauty discrimination" took place at a Kansas City television station. Christine Craft was demoted from her position as one of the nightly news anchors after her bosses decided that she was "too old, too unattractive, and not deferential to men." What that meant was, her male bosses disliked her style of dress, thought she didn't do enough to improve her appearance with make-up, and decided she didn't hide her intelligence well enough in order to make her male peers look smarter.

Craft insisted that the station's owner, Metromedia, Inc., reinstate her in the anchor job. Management refused, saying that their ratings had dropped because Kansas City viewers didn't like her. (In fact, the station became number one in the ratings after she was hired as an anchor.) Craft got a right-to-sue letter from the EEOC and took the station to court, charging them with sexual discrimination. The jury agreed, and awarded Craft half a million dollars in damages.

But the judge in the trial overruled the jury, and commanded that a new trial be held. The second jury also awarded Craft monetary damages. On appeal, however, the case was overturned, and the U.S. Supreme Court declined to review it. Interestingly, Justice Sandra Day O'Connor voted to review the case.

Craft's experience demonstrated how the competition for television ratings (and the ad dollars they bring in) can lead to an obsession with appearance. The news station didn't care how good a reporter Craft was—they only wanted a pretty woman to read copy over the airwaves.

Agism

Many Americans have been forced into retirement or turned down for new jobs because they are "too old." In most cases, employers want a younger person for either of two reasons: for appearances, or because health coverage for older employers is more

Most people over 65 are still fully competent to work at their jobs, or to begin new ones, but many are discriminated against because of their age.

expensive. Some firms may also feel that older workers are "slowing down" and therefore may be hurting productivity. Many experienced and healthy people over age 55 have run up against this form of discrimination. Worse yet, many employers are frank about their refusal to hire older people. Ironically, this comes at a time when companies are trying to do more business with fewer employees to cut costs. That means they need maximum work efficiency out of every employee. Younger, inexperienced workers may actually hurt this strategy.

A survey of male workers in the defense

industry concluded that despite their greater technical competence and education, older workers were the most likely to be laid-off or given "early retirement." Part of the reason for this is because after many years on the job, they are drawing large salaries. So discriminating against an older employee can mean reducing company expenses.

In the future, the reluctance of some companies to hire people over age 50, or even age 35, will fade fast as the population of the United States grows older. The baby boom generation is now approaching "middle age," and that means that by the year 2010 a large percentage of people in the United States will be at or near the classic retirement age of 65. So fewer and fewer young people will be available to fill job vacancies. Advertisers will have more older people to target, as more goods and services will be aimed at the aging population. Soon it will be impossible for companies to ignore the fact that the majority of consumers and workers who are still able and willing to be employed are over the now-outdated "retirement age."

The certainty that this country is aging, however, has not yet penetrated to all corners of our economy. So age discrimination continues, and it is very difficult to prove. Why it occurs is even more difficult to understand.

SIX

WHERE TO NOW?

It's been more than 35 years since Rosa Parks refused to move to the back of the bus. She would not give up her seat simply because she was born with dark skin.

In 1988, a black man ran for the Democratic Party's presidential nomination. The Reverend Jesse Jackson won so many delegates that he had to be considered a serious choice for the vice-presidential spot.

More than ever before, women around the globe are assuming leadership roles in politics, business, education and the military. For example, nations such as Great Britain, India, Pakistan, Nicaragua and the Philippines have been headed by female prime ministers and presidents. Females are demonstrating daily that they are just as good as males at any job. With these and many more positive changes, have we finally conquered the racism and sexism that creates discrimination?

Unfortunately, the answer is no. As just one example, read this finding from a recent national survey:

"Many whites believe blacks and other minorities are more violence-prone, less hard-working, less intelligent, less likely to be self-supporting and less patriotic than whites."

This was one conclusion of a 1990 poll taken by the National Opinion Research Center at the University of Chicago. On the positive side, the study also confirmed that a majority of white Americans support racial integration. So while Americans say they support equal opportunity, they also prefer to hold on to old stereotypes about minorities.

Prejudice and stereotypes are hard to shake. Even ethnic groups who have been victims of past discrimination are guilty of racist attitudes toward others. For example, in New York's Bensonhurst neighborhood, a young black man was killed by a white man in a racial incident. When blacks marched through the neighborhood in protest, they heard angry, racist remarks from the Italian-American residents. Many Italian-Americans experienced discrimination when they first came to the United States. They know that their parents, grandparents and great-grandparents were hurt by harmful names and discrimination. So why don't people recognize these same fears and sympathize with other victims of racism?

Why are hatred and discrimination so popular? Is racism learned from our parents and society, or do we just naturally suspect people who are different from us?

Discrimination And The Economy

The unfortunate reality is that discrimination has not been eliminated. Full equal opportunity does not yet exist. Consider this alarming U.S. Census Bureau statistic: White families are *ten times* wealthier than black families. In 1988, the average net worth for a black household was $4,170. For whites, it was $43,280 (net worth is the value of what you own, minus what you owe).

The biggest factor in this huge gap is the value of property. Homes and businesses owned by

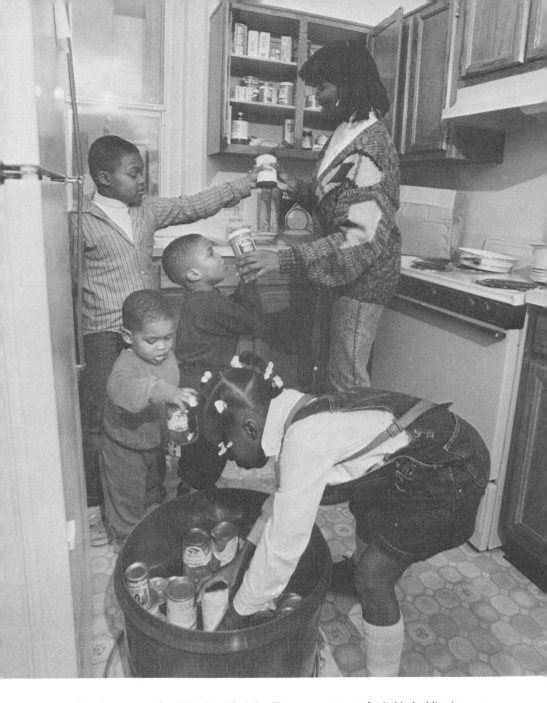

Despite progress in civil rights, black families on average are far behind whites in their net worth. The property values of homes owned by African-Americans are consistently far lower than homes owned by whites. Discrimination is the major factor.

white people are valued much higher than property owned by blacks. Blacks have less access to home and business loans, and their property values do not *appreciate* (or increase) at the same rate as white property. For example, in Washington, D.C., single-family houses in a mostly black neighborhood went up eight percent in value in five years. In a mostly white neighborhood in the same city, property values went up 99 percent during the same period.

The National Urban League (a black civil rights group) estimates that discrimination lowers the United States' gross national product by almost two percent, or more than $104 billion each year. Since the black work force is growing twice as fast as the white, the impact of this loss on our nation's financial health will only grow worse.

In a study of more than 10,000 small businesses in 28 U.S. cities, an economist found that loans to black businesses are almost 40 percent smaller than loans given to white borrowers with businesses of the same size.

When President Bush vetoed the Civil Rights Act of 1990, he become the first president ever to veto civil rights legislation. Bush said the new law would have forced businesses to adopt racial quotas to avoid lawsuits. Although many people believe he made the right decision, the timing of his veto was seen by many Americans to be a signal that minorities can expect less help from their government in fighting discrimination.

The racism that leads to discrimination can become expensive in surprising ways. For example, when the beating of a black man in Los Angeles was captured on videotape, the public outcry led to an investigation of the Los Angeles Police Department (LAPD) and police brutality. It turned out that the city of Los Angeles paid more than $8 million per year in settlements of lawsuits related to police brutality cases. So taxpayers' dollars were paying for the costs of these unfortunate events. The state of California also found that discrimination existed among the ranks of the LAPD in its treatment of black and Latino officers.

Affirmative action is often used as a "lightning rod" issue for political campaigns. That is, the words are loaded with positive and negative images, depending upon your opinion of affirmative action. In a 1990 North Carolina race, incumbent U.S. Senator Jesse Helms used television ads to imply that his opponent supported affirmative action. The ads asked if the voters were prepared to see job opportunities given to someone else. It was a clear appeal to those who feared that affirmative action was unfair to whites, and would lead to more unemployment. Although many people criticized Senator Helms' campaign for using a tactic that appealed to race (or racism), Helms still won reelection.

Affirmative action is not completely in retreat. For example, a 1990 Supreme Court decision permits Congress to set affirmative action policies that will increase broadcast licenses granted to women and minorities. Broadcast licenses are strictly controlled by the Federal Communications Commission (FCC), because the number of frequencies available on radio in any one geographic area is limited. Since only a few companies can broadcast at the same time, access is limited. The FCC is the watchdog that tries to make sure the airwaves fairly represent the community.

Is this broadcast ruling a quota, or a recognition that certain people have been disadvantaged in the past and must now be given more access to the radio airwaves? In this case, the court decision seems to "favor" minorities.

It has been more than a quarter century since the landmark Civil Rights Bill of 1964. Yet minority groups, legislators, voters, and lawyers continue to argue in courtrooms over the existence and effects of discrimination. If legislation has not significantly helped erase discrimination, are there other means available?

Money Talks

One very persuasive weapon in the war against racism is money. Some powerful organizations are using their financial power to try to mold or alter racial attitudes. For example, officials of the National Football League (NFL) felt they had to take a stand when the voters of Arizona repealed a law making Martin Luther King, Jr.'s birthday a state holiday. The NFL informed the state that the 1993 Super Bowl would not be played in Phoenix as planned unless the holiday was restored. The NFL felt that Arizona's voters were showing, at best, insensitivity to a national holiday so important to millions of Americans.

In March 1991, the NFL made good on its threat. The city of Phoenix (and the state in general) lost out on the many financial advantages of hosting a Super Bowl. This was the NFL's strategy: Restore the holiday, and we'll bring back the Super Bowl. Boycotts of this type may grow during the next decade as people decide to back up their beliefs with economic clout.

Bigotry And Free Speech

There is a growing movement on college campuses around the country to actively discourage bigotry toward others by suspending or expelling students who speak or act in a racist manner. For example, a student could be punished for displaying a sign in a dorm that contains racial slurs. But can limiting freedom of speech cure racism? Critics of these get-tough policies say this is nothing more than "thought control." It's more like washing someone's mouth out with soap than curing prejudice, or treating the symptoms instead of the disease.

Telling people they must not be prejudiced is no more effective than telling them they must not hate. You cannot change people's minds simply by telling them what they ought to think. Hatred can't be erased or forgotten with just a word or two. People have to be convinced that they are wrong, and even then, some won't change their attitudes. It's hard for human beings to give up beliefs that have given them simple explanations to complicated issues for years.

The Future

With all the barriers to human potential that still exist, it may seem silly to worry about methods of discrimination not yet invented. But is it? Scientific breakthroughs have recently provided the means to practice a new form of prejudice: *genetic* discrimination. There are already tests that allow greater accuracy predicting who will contract or inherit diseases, mental disorders and many cancers. This is not science fiction; these tests already exist. But will the widespread practice of a physical examination before hiring become a method to screen out those who *might* develop health problems?

This is not as farfetched as it sounds. For example, there have been cases of genetic discrimination related to sickle cell anemia, a blood disease common among black people. Certain jobs, such as that of airline pilot, have been denied to persons found to be "carriers"—someone who has the gene that causes the disease, but suffers no ill effects. This type of discrimination has already been challenged in the courts.

So concerned is the Congressional Office of Technology Assessment (OTA) about genetic job screening that it has started surveying companies to determine whether this practice is growing. With health care becoming more costly every day, companies are worried about having to insure someone with possible medical problems. They don't want to hire someone only to end up paying high medical bills if they become ill.

Insurance companies are also using medical testing to discover people having unusual health problems. Some states like California, however, have made it illegal for insurers to require tests for AIDS. Legislators felt that too many people were being unfairly denied basic medical insurance because they belonged to "higher risk" groups but did not actually have any illness.

Finding strength in our diversity—to appreciate and respect all types of people in the United States—is an elusive goal. But it is a goal worth striving for until all men, women and children are able to enjoy equal opportunity in peace.

Discrimination cannot be solved by changing human nature, and legal attempts to weed it out of society have only been partly successful. Does this mean that discrimination is something we "just have to live with"?

No. Any form of discrimination that prevents men, women and children from achieving their potential in this country deserves to be struck down and eliminated. If we don't try, then we are not really living up to the promise in the Bill of Rights, or in the words of Thomas Jefferson, to enjoy the right to "life, liberty, and the pursuit of happiness."

Glossary

AFFIRMATIVE ACTION. The policy of actively hiring and promoting women and members of minority groups to reverse the effects of past discrimination.

AGISM. Discrimination against people because they are older.

BOYCOTT. An organized protest where people refuse to deal with a business until some policy is changed.

CIVIL RIGHTS MOVEMENT. The period during the 1950s and 1960s when people marched, demonstrated and boycotted for equal rights for African-Americans.

CLASS ACTION SUIT. When a group of citizens combine their grievances in one lawsuit against a single organization.

COMPARABLE WORTH. The idea that different occupations are sometimes undervalued in the workplace. Some women want the same salary for jobs that come with the same responsibilities as some typically "male" jobs.

DESEGREGATION. To undo *segregation*, or enforced separation between two or more groups.

DISCRIMINATION. The act or policy of treating someone differently, keeping someone apart, or denying them his or her rights, simply because he or she is different from the majority.

EMANCIPATION PROCLAMATION. The executive order of President Lincoln declaring all slaves to be free men and women as of January 1, 1863.

EQUAL PROTECTION CLAUSE. The section in the 14th Amendment to the Constitution that prohibits discrimination against all citizens.

FEMINISM. The philosophy of equal rights for women.

INTEGRATE. To blend whites with minority groups, such as in school.

PREJUDICE. The fear and intolerance of other people because they do not belong to the same ethnic group, religion or gender as you.

QUOTAS. Setting a minimum number of persons to be hired and/or promoted solely to meet legal requirements of affirmative action.

REFUGEES. Adults and children who flee their native country to escape natural disasters like famine, or man-made problems like civil war.
REVERSE DISCRIMINATION. The phrase used by critics of affirmative action to describe the effects of these policies on white persons, particularly males.

SEGREGATION. The forced separation of races in a community.
SET ASIDES. see Quotas.
SEXUAL HARASSMENT. Insulting treatment by vocal abuse or physical contact, usually directed toward women.

UNALIENABLE RIGHT. A freedom that cannot be forfeited or transferred to someone else. (The word is also commonly spelled inalienable in today's usage.)

Bibliography

Clayton, Janet. "Shelby Steele." *Los Angeles Times*. January 13, 1991: M3.

Cooper, Jane. "Overweight and Under-Employed?" *Weight Watchers*. September 1990: 68-70.

Craft, Christine. "How 'the ugliest anchorwoman in America Battled Sexism in TV." *Chatelaine*. April 1988: 155-166.

Daniels, Gladys Rodriguez. "Americans with Disabilities Act." *Nation's Cities Weekly*. August 20, 1990: 5.

Everett, Martin. "Fat Chance." *Sales & Marketing Management*. March, 1990: 66-70.

Fulwood III, Sam. "Attitudes on Minorities in Conflict." *Los Angeles Times*. January 9, 1991.

Hoopes, Roy. "Working Late: On the outside looking in." *Modern Maturity*. June-July 1989: 32-39.

Lynch, Frederick R. "Surviving Affirmative Action (More or Less)." *Commentary*. August 1990: 44-47.

Mann, Judy and Basia Hellwig. "The Truth About the Salary Gap(s)." *Working Woman*. January 1988: 61-62.

McGuire, Leslie. *The Family: Death And Illness*. Vero Beach, FL: Rourke Publishing, 1990.

Meier, Gisela. *Women Today: Minorities*. Vero Beach, FL: Rourke Publishing, 1991.

Steele, Shelby. "The Recoloring of Campus Life."
    Harper's Magazine. February 1989: 42-55.

Updegrave, Walter L. "Race and Money." *Money*.
    December 1989: 152-172.

"A Working Woman's Guide To Her Job Rights." U.S.
    Dept. of Labor, Women's Bureau. June 1988:
    Leaflet 55.

The World Almanac and Book of Facts 1991. New
    York: Pharos Books, 1991.

Zamichow, Nora. "Isolation Painful for Partners of
    Gays in Service." *Los Angeles Times*, February
    3, 1991: A9, 12.

INDEX

Picture Credits